Accompanying the Sun

Portraits in Poetry

Accompanying the Sun

Portraits in Poetry

Duncan A. Rouch

Hotham Hill Publishing

Hotham Hill Publishing

© 2020, Duncan A. Rouch

duncanrouch@gmail.com

ISBN: 978-0-6484664-5-1

Contents

Forward

This is my second book of poetry, following the 'Eye of the Storm King' poetry book, with similar themes. These are, a type of 'praise poetry', connected to the idea that it would useful to acknowledge the positive characteristics of people, and a type of 'challenge poetry', to reflect on challenges that people face in life, from both internal and external issues, often to have an emotionally darker feel, though often with at least a little light open for hope.

If any of these poems bring up related difficulties for you, please consider calling your relevant local mental health helpline. Listed in the appendix are selected helpline numbers for Australia, New Zealand, United Kingdom, and the USA.

Local and/or General

Electric Blue

The helter-skelter life of a woman on the run from childhood trauma

Bright flash of her electric blue eyes as we laugh in the long grass
Wild fall of Titian red curls lilt with her assured supple motion
Smart thoughts rise swiftly above the clinging parochial suburb
Quick her escape to the medical world iridescent as opal

Success her star in this impersonal professional career
Yet a marriage erased in the endless search for enduring love
Her bloody scratch as she reaches to caress the feral cat
Without tears each frustration locked in the transit hold of mind

The frightened penniless boy she befriends at the city bus stop
Thanks in halting English bless her for securing his ticket home
The morose widower gilded in tears she comforts on the bus
To demand intense attention the lonely man trails her home

Escape by hang-glider ends in broken limbs amidst the daisies
Held still in the white bed tests tag her fractured beauty with cancer
No reprieve from the dark corrosive crucible of inner tension
Restless thoughts turn in pain to the imprisoned trauma of childhood

Outside the young magpie flexed its wings in the swirling Spring storm
The house of unspokeness held her numb at the death of father
Her youthful head pregnant with the push of his distant perfection
Doomed to search for the nourishment of love he never offered her

Compassion voluptuous as the rose signals her unloved heart
In meditation the deep peace to weave past error into self
From oily depths her spirit emerges into clear calm water
In tranquil blue eyes the strength to bear life's weight or death's release

Accompanying the Sun

A blind girl engages with life

Laughing emerald orbs add only to her winsome beauty
Invisible to her the morning star rise across cerulean sky
Yet she can read you like a news stand flyer on Ryrie Street
You are open as a bright Irish jig or dark Bach cantata

Chocolate and your happy dog light her bright smile and lively laugh
Splintered dimensions of conversation reveal the real you
Taste the tart of subtext passenger with the souffle of silence
By these signs across the aether she sees the state of your karma

Exhilarating dash with her through Spencer Street Station subway
Her assured motion accompanies the sun in your wetland walk
Halt to hear the call of plumed egrets over susurrant reeds
Reason rises from the tempo of your footsteps across soft sand

Storm Leader

The balance of feminine and masculine strengths in a strong leader

Unwavering cobalt blue eyes cast calmness as the storm descends
In this pell-mell business push she strong as the gunmetal sea
Fair as the full moon as the restrained win-win negotiator
Eloquently she draws the play against fate fault and fallacy

At home the menagerie of pets responds to her love and care
One tenth of her income sent against poverty and injustice
By murmuring brook she dryly tells the trauma of lost friendship
His gentle question uncovers pain of trust brutally betrayed

At the coffee shop vulnerable brightness describes a new friendship
For the fretful child of the friend she sings a lilting lullaby
Quiet admission of fear for her vomit compounded with blood
Quick to restore cobalt blue eyes cast calmness as the storm descends

Vorsprung Durch Technick

Leni Riefenstahl (1902-2003), dictator Hitler's film director

In the crisp avenue of air the red eye calls an orderly halt
Repeated heated quaver of my car horn insists instant movement
I ego tower over the wave of suburban submarines
In the prison of impulse I a metre short of the impulse shop

Neatly buried like Poland the maelstrom of my distant childhood
Capricious roller coaster tied to an alcoholic mother
Each tense day I breathless as the high jumper thrown over a cliff
I emerge the svelte blonde intense cobalt blue eyes ever restless

In that other time hot tears until dawn in grief of love shattered
I flee failure of the heart in cool technique of the film maker
In Hitler's shining ascendance I see the star of destiny
Invincible Wehrmacht and adoring Volk my film creation

Capricious roller coaster of the Nazi blitz to dominion
Truth slips from my slim grasp as the ever fleeting sundrop of praise
Craving the intimate caress by the panther of power
As he emerges I stand breathless in the avenue of air

At war's end I see a soldier hurl his iron cross in grey mud
Thrust too in my sight the crumpled photograph of a lost daughter
Her dulcet Jewish beauty surely damned in a distant death camp
On air avenue the wind whispers Sieg Heil Sieg Heil Sieg Heil

Sensuous

The five senses in action

In gentle sparring talk the joyous glow of her eye captures I
Through vivid slate blue see the rich depths of her vivacious spirit

As she walks hush of black stocking brushed by tracery-trimmed skirt
In this rhythm I hear her ever compassion to assuage lost souls

Supple fingers render origami from a wild plastic bag
In deft touch the warm precision of her sharp full-fledged intellect

Delight aflame by tumultuous flavours of a home set meal
Bold full-bodied battery of books booms a woman of high taste

Soft aroma of her perfume follows I as the rising moon
This scent recalls the pleasure to voyage through her silken space

The Chocolate Cake

The sensuality of chocolate

Patiently he awaits my gaze in the glittering shop window
Perfect arc of his soft form and sweet aroma raise my pulse
Ever handsome in silky dark skin he basks voluptuously
His luxuriant body a delectable double layer

Swiftly he does all that I ask without grimace or grating word
Pregnant silence falls as he travels home in my fervent embrace
He floats aglow on the glass table yet cool to my bold caress
This tumultuous affair casts my old life in jagged fragments

In the tense grasp for control I deliver the ultimatum
Yet adorned by his alluring smile he refuses to depart
Glint of knife in my trembling hand yet he arrogantly unmoved
Breathlessly I consume the evidence to the last rich morsel

Worder

Portrait of an editor

Soft spiral locks in rich array frame fine featured beauty
Deep eye and pursed lips mark powerful concentration on the word
Relentlessly she delivers the diamond of clarity
Imprisoned beneath the mud-encrusted surface of crumbled prose

Under her spell the many word of book and succinct word of play
Brief word of newspaper and mellifluent word of magazine
In eye of camera the immediate word of broadcast news
Her vivacious spirit brings bold life to word of a dying world

Jackie

Jacqueline Du Pré (1945-1987), famed cello player

Mellifluous music of the gods flowers from supple fingers
Her brittle comet blazes across grey skies to pristine delight
Youthful limbs embrace the warm ancient wood her tempestuous slave
She thirsts for the seductive love of an enraptured audience

Childhood lost in the brute push of a mother's veiled ambition
Present departed in useless search for an ordinary touch
Future laid to dust with sense and muscle crushed by cruel disease
Dancing as her fingers sun-dappled poplars susurrate her name

Ashes of a Man

In memory of Arch Roberts (1910-2002)

Fractious Winter storm abates by the bay in this sentient hour
Assembled family and friends contemplate a life well fulfilled
Spiritual words in gentle rhythm assets for this atheist
Open to inner peace as the light breeze bathes the ancient pier

Two youths of the bloodline cast out the ashes of this beloved man
Bright shower of fine powder fans over the soft afternoon sea
Here carbon nitrogen phosphorus and essential metals
Nurturing by this ash the bold symbol of life laid from a life

Gardener of the mind as great as his lush verdant home haven
Quiet confidence fronts strong array of contemplative talents
Worlds transformed through the measured painter's hand and camera eye
From the creative muse maturity brings eccentric concepts

Muse measured methods by noble analytical chemistry
Professional days recall acts with balance ash and mercury
To her he gentle companion dependable as the Spring tide
Beyond ancient pier sunlight dances over the peaceful swell

Beach at Sixteen

The low mackerel Spring sky above reflects the red rising orb
On golden sand receding tide leaves perfect diamond arrays
Rock pools like obsidian clear to the ripple sandy bottom
Explosion of water as she jumps through oblivious to I

Pearls fall from her aqueous locks to frame superior knowing
Unseen to I her brash shield of conceit yet the flash of excited smile
As she rotates to depart her strong steady eye liberates I
She strides of with her black dog as buxom brunette in red wetsuit

From the lookout sun dappled hills fall into the gunmetal sea
As she laughs with him and I her gaze alights I then spin away
By the low bridge arc her tears yet smouldering glare bars I from aid
Silence at the sienna shimmer across dusky broad water

Rainbow missive a bold invitation to her birthday party
The Adrian Henri poems I give her are lost in the glitz
I push her best friend in the river to steal her attention
Her eyes flash in anger as sunrays dancing on foam-flecked surf

Grace

How can I regret one moment in your aerial realm
Deft precision of your will selfless as graceful French lace
In luxuriant array slim spirals of hair shimmer
A smile to bring the sun over the endless cerise sea

Camellia petals fall over velvet skin aglow
Tender line of this vivacious incandescent mind
Your silky silhouette commands the high cornflower sky
Finely tempered motion whispers exhilarating grace

Boxhill

A victim of violence rebuilds her life

All I ask the soft Summer breeze lilting leaves high on Boxhill
Arms out like White Admiral in wistful lightness of being
Sadness shade due only to ending of the beautiful day
Not once more can happy innocence return to that warm moment

Behind the counter I the shop girl masked by a brittle smile
Burnished copper locks hide acrid tears in the quiet hour
How was it I to lie blood-soaked and broken on cold hard ground
Now measured tone the voice to control self-hatred of this victim

In court these modest walking shoes evidence that I not the whore
Prison once again for him tight life as the hard hollow lad
I to rebuild self redeeming dream of love with a special man
On Boxhill among dappled leaves my shadow a more solid form

Lasseter

Lewis Hubert (Harold Bell) Lasseter (1880-1931), self-made man who perished in the search for a mythical gold reef in central Australia

At dawn tranquil frost covered red earth of his desert tomb
This marks the last push for success to appease a restless spirit
Determined as the desert sun to forge success of each project
Long reach of unspoken grief at mother's swift death when he a child

At each new direction a new self created to aid the cause
Effervescent confidence that the new man would bring bright triumph
Yet results often fell below the bar of high expectation
Depression cast darkly as the heavy velvet sky at twilight

Gathered the potential investors for his ultimate scheme
Bold means to assuage the added burden of failure at fifty
Intense the story told of a rich gold reef beyond the sandhills
Depression Australia wanted to believe it to be real

Pan his story to find truth hidden like small gold flecks in dense dirt
Here said that he himself had seen the reef thirty years before
He had exchanged himself for the originator of the tale
A subterfuge to render this tale real to he and audience

From Alice Springs the six expeditioners trekked west in high hope
His deep edginess emerged as they approached the truth of his tale
Prickly as the Spinifex his ego pared the team down to one
At Shaw Creek arid sand of the bed desiccated as his throat

In delirium he sees the reef's seven miles glorious of gold
Datum peg hammered hard to the quiescent quartz renders the claim
Aborigines perceive a dying man lost beyond their aid
Last diary entries testament to a self misunderstood

Unknown the Road – Know the Self

In memory of Karen Willets (1968-2003)

Summer light mottled on the willow shaded cool Cherwell waters
With friends languid ripples from the punt reflect her delightful smile
Soft breeze ruffles rich sienna curls about her fine Georgian face
On grassy bank in calm repose her quiet strength like the river

In laboratory her perseverance with the life factor
Its precious nourishment of developing nerve and lung tissue
Sureness sparks in her young eye cast with a thread of uncertainty
To Marseilles she delves mysteries of the acrid AIDS virus

Back to this southern haven for community-minded science
Smooth run yet slowing trajectory on the unknown road of life
Unknown self she impelled on the restless search for inner peace
Turn off in hope to Buddhist realm yet too hungry to see the signs

Each perceived failure in life a cataclysmic failure of self
Fatally the unloved self believed she to be unlovable
Not learnt the base skill to negotiate the black ice of crisis
Beyond shaded water her perfect form lies at eternal peace

The Woman Who Knew

*A journalist good at reporting news of the world has difficulty understanding her
self*

This woman of bold substance, svelte reporter of the hidden truth
Arrays of contacts leaven the search for provocative story
Through interview empathy impels astute query to flesh fact
Her self ever renewed in the crucible of unique experience

Yet refractive to enquiry the hidden secrets of the self
Accumulated at impenetrable depth long banished raw pain
Fast life relaxed to form the orchid of meditative repair
Luxuriant foliage and bloom emerge from her patient care

Quicksilver

Portrait of a scientist

Spare timeless beauty abounds as elegant as the Great Egret
She unfolds her wings to swing vibrantly across the rising sun
Warm her smile as she passes by in ever aesthetic motion
A mind as bright as quicksilver explores unknown territory

The deep sea of food chemistry her glittering destination
First bold analysis the stability of Canola oil
She probes below the surface to catch the fundamental science
Silver water reflects her lithesome form rising toward the stars

Open Heart

In her open home a resonant throng delights in sense of place
Around the bold lotus these the needful beloved, friend and stranger

From her ever open heart rises the white dove of empathy
Vibrant conversation reforms to the warm word in sustenance

Her open spirit riven from bright love and personal darkness
Within her eye the swan of grace adorns the deep rock of patience

After The Rain

Portrait of a teacher

Her measured dulcet voice rings out clear as the valley after rain
Flash of her smile amidst raven locks liberally woven in curves
Enthusiastic teacher guiding young minds to scale mountain height
Above a dappled mackerel sky glows red in the setting rays

In a modest moment her sprightly eyes turn down in silent sense
Graceful hands cross as her face shines vibrantly with the new challenge
Inside knowledge she imparts about deep mysteries of the cell
Beyond juvenile magpies race about arboreal splendour

True Rebel

Portrait of an anarchist

Dark shock of curly locks with bold moustache frame vibrant sapphire eyes
Once an ordinary boy floundering by the low side of town
His rough spirit broke through the ashen weight of poor expectation
This man who gained independence through bright chaotic rebellion

Swan of success at University after told impossible
Began his own company with inside knowledge of computers
Strained the ill-fitting anarchist's suit as his identity mask
Yet selflessly helped the schizophrenic man gain a normal life

This rebel with buried trauma disrupting his rise from the ash
A myriad parking fines accumulating like a time bomb
For the unemployed and others down repaired computers for free
On freeway the big red box of his old car speeds relentlessly

Conversation by the Sea

By the restless silver sea stands the large white house adorned in green
Airy canvases mark the residence of the absent painter
Youthful acquaintances arrive for an effervescent weekend
Strong sunlight and deep arboreal shade under the wide Southern sky

Along faded wooden pier a small group rambles to reach dark rocks
In open silence she and he remain to watch from weathered rail
Bright call of yellow robins amid rustle of wind through tea trees
Hesitant rhythm of first conversation gently emerges

Tranquil she surveys a wide future from final year school
Quite certainty in the face of scant experience in life
Reflective he out on the doubt swept pier of an uncertain career
Ever restless waves mirror the imprisoning inner turmoil

From careful thought she builds a lean bridge to reach practical choice
Bold action denied for he clocked by fear of unknowingness
Lucid conversation spaced as gentle puffs of the shifting wind
From distant end of ash grey pier light flocks of laughter emanate

Harper

Based on the character of Harper in 'Angels in America', HBO films (2003)

Like Schopenhauer I sometimes wonder if happiness exists
My life a transparent vessel empty bar slim scraps of success
This outer skin of the dutiful wife becomes claustrophobic
Behind I a hollow childhood constrained as the perfect daughter

Dreams weaved of world travel as I fight the raven of depression
Suffocating comfort in the bright luxuriant apartment
Eventual desperate escape to crisp snow cloaked Central Park
I imagine gliding blissfully through grand Alaskan forest

At dusk the return home confused with this heart bearing light numbness
His words form new arrays of chains to enclose this growing spirit
My voice scratches the air in vain attempt to bring understanding
In this close embrace his cold eyes shut hard to recall another

By the door my slim suitcase and calm resolve to depart that man
The lush hills of northern India call for trek of this spirit
Rising flight eastward painted by golden rays of the rising sun
I with peaceful heart step onto the unknown path to future self

Bold Pursuit

In honour of French vulcanologists Maurice Kraft (1946-1991) and Katia Kraft (1942-1991)

Their quest to observe the fiery fundamental forces of earth
Natural powers that shaped this planet from its tumultuous birth
He and she dedicated to document volcanic action
Majestic signals of the great continental plates in motion

Ever courage in close arrival to intense volcanic heat
Inspiration for a generation of young earth scientists
Their array of films too a great aid for public understanding
Their lives extinguished by massive pyroclastic flow of debris

Across the globe their silent home amongst arboreal splendour
This low room open like the captain's cabin of a windjammer
Burgeoning shelves of books chart bold scientific pursuit
Beyond this wood-panelled realm of science the bright breeze bells their names

Photograph

By the hard white bed the bright family photograph
Happiness adorns the healthy faces by his birthday candles
Under sheet his body stripped to a thirty kilograms shadow
Bone cancer has roughly taken his manly protection from her

Shattered china across the kitchen floor in soft Autumn sunlight
Dappled rays finds her head bowed in grief yet no release in tears
The crucible of anger within denies her old tranquillity
In her fractured face the jolt of a journey only just begun

Comfort of Snow

To recall the lost generation of Aboriginal children, Australia

Flash of a melancholy smile framed by arrayed coal ringlet locks
Havana brown skin of her perfect hand on the white cotton bag
Her dark doleful eye tells a life hit by endless fleets of brute kicks
Inner scares an enduring hallmark of the lost generation

Jettisoned into the cruel half-life existence between cultures
Racist taunt from white flotsam explodes as sharp shrapnel in her face
Denied heritage by the word of a pure Koori descendent
Yet her nascent spirit holding out against the deadening tide

Depressed escape to the high country to reach the comfort of snow
Calmness envelops her in the measured fall of pristine snowflakes
Inner strength builds in the soft tranquil contemplation of past pain
Her spirit to boldly soar as the brown goshawk over white slope

Franklin

In memory of Rosalind Franklin (1920-1957), forgotten scientist

Her vibrant mind only satisfied with the difficult questions
Patience of French lace and perseverance against all obstacles
Technical prowess from attention to the ultimate detail
Scientific proof through acquiring precise data her lodestone

Silent tension haunts the corridors in King's College of London
Conflict with Wilkins smouldering from ill-matched expectations
She her independence of work and mind under a crucial threat
He unable to perceive the different needs of his star charge

Step on step casting no chance to be destroyed by man or science
Anxiety at the high stakes renders her nervous presentations
Her measured deftness in the dark room to expose the great image
Beauty in symmetry of the stepped cross framed by opposing arcs

Watson combative at her steady work though she most unmovable
Bar sharp comment she holds back by the reserve of feminine strength
She berates Watson for wildly building castles high in the sky
Compassion constrains her frustration at limits in the male world

In 1952 her strong mastery of X-ray technique
The majestic diffraction portraits of DNA hers alone
Patience in endless calculations to reveal the hidden truth
Her essential part in unmasking the riddle of DNA

The Map Maker

Dedicated to Sue Longmore, Australian campaigner to help asylum seekers
Reference: 'You're The Voice', song by John Farnham, 1991

On camera her thoughtful words as gentle as the morning rays
Patience in her bold task to reveal hidden lives of the interned
The kaleidoscope of world experience held behind barbed wire
To them her parcel sent bearing simple shapes of brightly hued cloth

Her purpose for these people to write of sadly afflicted lives
In reply on each cloth shape inscribed escape from torment and hope
Assembling the shapes begins to reveal a map of this great land
To complete the map arrays of broken lives call our compassion

American Chimaera

A white man finds solace in taking on the identity of an American Indian

Steady eye awaits then flash of his spear to catch the glowing Perch
Strong arms paddle the canoe across dancing glitter of the lake
Beyond the sandy shore his log hut alone amongst the Oak wood
Tough pelt clothes adorned by Night Hawk feathers and beads of earthen hues

Chimaeric as a bronzed-skin Indian with an inner white soul
Like the gentle fall of autumn leaves he shed his most western ways
His past hidden in darkness as the ground deep in the Pine forest
Born the unloved child of that alcoholic mother in Coketown

Delinquent violence brings quick recognition by the boys' gang
Saturday night drug-store robbery slammed his body in jail
A restless mind brought to contemplation of bleakest future end
Muttered by a broken Mohican the fragments of a noble life

This ancient dream his hollow self imbibes over disastrous past
To be an element at one with the prime milieu of nature
Fulfilment to love hawk and hickory bright lovers in return
At dawn the Wood-Thrush and Blue-Jay sing for his ever enjoyment

Under the Summer sun he emerges as the Indian Ranger
By canoe to lead families to love the natural treasures
Forty Winters on his lifeless form found at peace by the blue ice
Still shade of Oak and ripple of water recall this quiet man

Opal Eyes

Falling wave of dark locks mirrors her svelte form in gentle motion
Within opal eyes the supple strength of the quiet Mountain Ash
As she glides in empathy hand and foot in tranquil synchrony
In work together thoughts exchange in silent cooperation

Her bright spirit slides high into the enormous cerulean sky
On barren ground a lesson in opening the orchid of trust
A mind to marshal resources for teaching practical science
By the silver sea she contemplates the ties of bold compassion

Betrayal

In honour of Beth Heinrich, survivor of sexual abuse

His religion a sparkle in the pulpit yet only skin deep
A mind as impulsive as the wind across the Lachlan Valley
Little care of consequence heralds the dark trail of destruction
Loud glory in the moment reflects an ego unbound by truth

She the child of ordinary need to trust and follow guidance
In her youthful eyes the malleable innocence his ego chose
Sex on the fox-skin rug amid petals of empty promise
Fuel for her dream of husband and children blessed in God's domain

His black panic at her gentle request for bright promise fulfilled
Upon his false accusation she sent home in cruel dark disgrace
Confusion in her seared heart yet in love with the life he promised
Shared intense emotion chained her hard to this handsome hollow man

For her a life obscenely betrayed in the search for fulfilment
Bereft of moral he unable to fall faithful to any one
For him a life as meaningful as jetsam on Lachlan River
By the Newell Highway great fields of wheat whisper her deep torment

True Love

Before the dawn I creep barefoot up through wiry scrub to cliff's edge
Behind me gentle rustle of gnarled Tea Trees in the Autumn breeze
In stillness I wait for my true love's ship to round the wind-swept spit
So long since his last letter embellished with the bright hope of Spring

Each written word a rich refracting jewel from a distant heart
The golden promise of deep happiness in simple dreams fulfilled
Home a cottage of wattle and daub with an ever welcome hearth
Children to share heartache and joy in this rough-cut new colony

Majestically a Currawong glides by in growing Eastern light
Below by surf-specked rocks Shearwater and Gull hunt for silver fish
Too soon the sun's arc rises to cast dappled arboreal shadows
Once more a day bereft of him yet I wait in assured lightness

Havana Eyes

With one svelte foot on the chair she stands to check the answer machine
Her petite beauty held in straight lines by the chestnut business suit
A deep voice braced in the steady rhythm of quiet authority
This feminine self cast amongst that industry built of big men

Slim-cut brunette locks adorn a head made for figures and detail
Her office spare in immaculate form ready for swift action
To work alone brings clarity of deep thought and bright endeavour
Among the throng Havana eyes sparkle in empathic discourse

Love Renewed

In the fresh light of Spring the radiant couple stand in soft embrace
He the handsome Chesterfield engineer adorned by sharp moustache
She vivacious brunette became astute Fleetways' organiser
As the white clouds deftly race westward her faience blue eyes flash love

This world man out to aid all leaves promise of home tasks unfulfilled
Brother and sister answered before she the bright wife and mother
Her strong will casts the searing crisis before his Havana eyes
Within her tender eyes the bright threads of hope for love reconciled

Tear on tear as his life cut by the relentless knife of cancer
On her head bowed in grief alights fragrant blossom of the sweet pear
With five children aglow in spirit she must begin life once more
In rise of the daffodil she recalls the first time he held her

The Microbiologist

In honour of Dr John May, microbiologist

This softly spoken scientist with the deceptively light touch
Dive deep with his knowledge into the physiology of the cells
From African beer yeast to the polyphosphate bacterium
Vivacious Adam and Eve his veteran self-built fermenters

With him share the thrill to delve wondrous mysteries of the microbe
To adorn bare perseverance with a rich measure of passion
In his bright eye the glint reveals the tough voyage to self-knowledge
Beloved teacher and mentor his warm care known by generations

Incandescent Eye

In honour of Dr Tim Littlejohn, information technologist

Only the computer matched the hyperactive science student
White dawn of excitement in a million possible applications
Opportunity seized like Icarus to boldly fly skyward
The Internet mirrors the virtual web of his arrayed contacts

In his cerulean eye the incandescent fusion of the sun
To build the bright future from a thousand invisible ideas
High arcs span biology to business via computing
Each day he rides the rich maelstrom of chaotic construction

Passion to inform us about the biodiversity push
Deep identity from home as equal partner and fair father
Time in the quiet moments to re-sustain bright extrovert self
In Summer light the Currawong glides through arboreal splendour

Give a Little Bit of Love

Who needs careless friends?
Reference: 'Give a Little Bit', song by Supertramp (1977)

Short dense jet curls in rich array frame a rough handsome vibrant face
Cobalt blue eyes flash constant readiness to act first before thought
Compulsive fervour in beer, cigarette and loveless one-night-stands
A self brittle as Winter pond ice ready to argue and fight

This bright trail leads backward to a forgotten loveless childhood
A father long left him to the hard alcohol-damaged mother
Heavy on him the roller coaster of dark emotion and blame
Attention by her hard eye that brutal vanguard to acid words

A Winter Saturday night in town to drink with two married friends
Return to their cool Moss Side flat for further ale and argument
At 1 am he falls hard in drunken coma by the table
Without a care they retire to their bed and electric blanket

His erratic breathing as the room cools this bleak frost-riven night
Useless shiver as heart-beat slows perilously in this cold space
Helpless to escape the lethal attack of hypothermia
Shrill call of Robin at dawn and his once restless form still in death

Rainbow Serpent

Trek with a custodian of Arnhem Land, Australia

Watch and GPS superfluous like the baggage in his head
Expert knowledge in lay of wind hue of sea and season of plant
This sufficient to find sustenance and water in Arnhem Land
Stars of the seven brothers guide his sienna canoe to shore

To sleep on the silver sand to evade sharp arboreal insects
Honey from bright orange fingered flower of the Grevillea
Through water quick eye and patient spear hunt the hidden stingray
Fast friction begins the drift wood fire to braze the sumptuous catch

Crocodile spirit guards his canoe amongst the shady mangroves
Tasty Docray shell and mangrove worm revealed to his fast hand
In walk from swamp senses alight to read rich detail of the land
On almond green hills barefoot hike sideways over sharp edged grass

By the standing rock he offers green branches to favour the hunt
At the ancient cave by rainbow serpent his mark of white clay hand
Meditation in this calm spiritual space centres his spirit
In the clear eye of this young Yolngu man light of a bright future

Man of Flowers

A tribute to Norman Kaye (1927-2007), Australian film actor and musician

To reveal bouquets of truth as the king or fool, priest or lover
The fragile self encouraged to flower in a dry barren world
Travelling through the inner and outer dimensions of our selves
Fearless in performance from a built belief in the strength of self

Calmed the demons from broken family repressed in poverty
First escape in music by the soaring power of the organ
Back in Melbourne emerges the catalytic and creative actor
Arrays of cinnabar sprays adorn the luxuriant fire-wheel tree

Blooming partnership with the enigmatic young film director
The white rose of trust among the red orchids of integrity
This inventive explosion of bold complementary passions
To exuberantly explore the rich fertile land of our dreams

Spirit of North Melbourne

In memory of John Castle (1934-2006), Australian football trainer

The bright sun rises in the clear cerulean sky this Autumn day
Energizing breeze rides sharply over the North Melbourne hill
In blue and white match trim they emerge from the byways for the game
He a trainer is at the Arden Street ground to help set the team

Self-belief enforced to beat the challenge of osteomyelitis
Discreet confidant of players burdened by weight on the mind
Nurtured belief in the heart that brings their talent to spark on field
Joy in the circle to vociferously voice the great club song

He of the old town in close brick cottages and hotels aplenty
To uphold the grand traditions of mateship and robust drinking
Pride ever in the bright eyed endeavours of the bold footballers
Through word and action this man marks the strong spirit of North Melbourne

Sleek form of the classic white Ford Falcon car brings he and her home
To appreciate leaf and petal in home rounds as the gardener
In crisis stubborn as steel yet selfless in support of the team
Ever on game day the Northern spirit will come down from the hill

Deception 1

Hollowness of a television reality show

Selves dissolve under the intense watch of one hundred cameras
This reality television show renders them as soft porn players
Each vacuous wanton woman bears buxom breasts barely restrained
Their youthful faces adorned by bright blush of back-street night hookers

Puerile purine brings boredom gauche adolescent motion
In 'cheer leader' practice empty eyes glazed as cheap automatons
Brains hibernate by the pool as bodies shine for the camera
Her escape to humiliation on the television chat show

Mellifluous self returns as the happy vibrant girl-next-door
Glorious golden locks frame her trusting face like the morning sun
Corn-flower blue eyes emit warm dynamic sensitivity
Captivating rugged rhythm of her words reveal a subtle truth

Deception 2

Jodie Harris, convicted con artist

Afternoon sun brings a translucent glow to the spacious old room
By the lemon-painted wall the 1950's designer couch
Stillness yet beyond the picture window leaves dance in the cool breeze
Tireless ticking of a clock marks the time since she left forever

Too young for her parents incarcerated as drug users
Rebellious as too old to be placed in the warm foster care home
Stealing lipstick for attention placed her in the police station
A mute smile in deep admiration of the smart policewoman

Her brash action hides the hurt of a disconnected cold childhood
In false identity a safe distance from dark inner turmoil
Easy to ride through the naive trust of the lonely well-to-do
Swiftly she enters the bank to harvest material self-reward

Vivacious self brings close relationship with the young policeman
She yearns for emotional shelter and a cheerful steady life
Yet this link precipitates handcuffs and a cold cell without him
Time to heal the buried scars of childhood and reveal her true self

Death of a Mother, part I

*In memory of Dianne Brimble (1960-2002), who died from date-rape drugs
aboard a holiday cruise ship in 2002*

Over the tranquil verdant garden warm rain flecks steadily fall
Driving drops transduced to circular ripples on the lily pond
Glossy the moist surface of the grey stone tiles laid neatly by
Soft tumble of clear water gliding under the small wooden bridge

Brightly her buxom feminine self steps across the wet garden
She opens in a ready smile like the vivacious camellia
Within dark eyes trials of life behind the effervescent joy
A gentle spirit looking for trust and compassion in others

On the cruise of a lifetime with daughter and girlfriend's family
Long she dreamed of this exciting voyage on bright tropical seas
Sensual escape with base beat rhythm on the warm vibrant dance floor
Flattered by conversation with the coterie of brash bold men

Unaware her drink was spiked with gamma hydroxy butyrate
Will and sense held captive by this darkly hazardous date-rape drug
In a docile haze she led swaying to their small grimy cabin
A night of sexual and drug violation without her consent

The lethal twist of dangerous chemicals bound within her blood
Her naked comatose form left to perish on the cabin floor
With a mournful cry the Great Frigatebird of trust left the white ship
Over the tranquil verdant garden warm rain flecks steadily fall

Death of a Mother, part II

*In memory of Dianne Brimble, 1960-2002. How the self-centred life of a man led
to her death*

In the fogbound road rays of streetlights barely penetrate the night
He sees a homeless boy loitering beyond the gate of his house
With angry shouts he chases the boy along the derelict road
His large fist forces the slim boy hard head-first against sharp gravel

-----

For the camera he smiles anticipation with seven mates
Sex alcohol and drugs this hedonistic crew plan on board
D Deck cabins their grey base place on the white Pacific Sky ship
Hollow egos give heavy jolt motion on the disco dance floor

His steel eyes tracked the laughing buxom woman across the warm space
Conversation in his smiling mask reeled her in as a fish
His mates arrogantly conspired in this abusive tawdry game
To break her will with selfish pleasure he secretly spiked her drink

Her right to consent barred by his goal of self-gratification
She to be perilously submissive to his swollen ego
Her bright inner beauty beyond his threadbare empathy to know
In confusion she led away to the dirty D Deck cabin

Drugged and sexually attacked her form discarded on grey floor
Coldly pushed out by the narcissist to die without love or care
Two-faced he denounced her as ugly black with vile feminine smell
Her supine form silently signalled for help yet remained ignored

In The Air

Interpretation of the song 'In The Air Tonight', by Phil Collins (1981)

Out in the dry Hakea forest I've felt your corrosive presence
Your name voiced in the leaves' susurrus answer to the west force wind
Arrival in the storm with your dirty coat and hair in wet mess
Deep in my mind I know your every gauche move and ugly thought

Each day I see your ego puts pitiful errors of judgement
I arrogantly wait for the moment when you pull out the gun
You as the hollow man addicted to the adrenalin rush
Don't worry, I am the expert private detective on your case

This hard grey prison cell calls out the deep dark demons in your head
In the small cracked mirror I see your angry broken drug-etched face
That grime-coated reflection clearly resolves that you are I
In the acrid prison air hangs the slim thread of my redemption

Under the Milky Way

From the light smiling baby emerged this quiet young woman
Her slim form smartly adorned by the bright coral red party dress
Softly spoken she slowly reads her story to the gathering
Bright emotion in expressing the feisty life of her grandmother

In her dark eyes sensibility of a sentient being
To knowingly bear the burden of the one extra chromosome
Simply aberrant expression of some genes for the face and mind
Delight in each modest flexing of her wings for independence

Nurtured by close ties of parental care weighted by self knowledge
Together the hot tears and bold laughter of each precious day
Arm in arm their measured walk through the luxuriant silent garden
Under the Milky Way eternal bonds of love and compassion

In The Car With Joan Baez

Newport Folk Festival ~1964

Her unique soprano tones float through the Newport Festival air
Elemental song accompanied by the guitar on her knee
Deftly she brings to sweet life the timeless folk ballads and laments
Warm applause from the smiling young crowd cast on the cool Summer grass

Away in the car her slim face framed in the passenger window
Her dark sparkling eyes carry passion for human and civil rights
Outside the sterile row of grey tree-less identical houses
In this small space the blooms of bright conversation and compassion

Coryli's Challenge

A young woman battles with a mental health issue

Golden locks dyed mouse brown to help hide her amongst the scenery
Nervously she sits in silence near the back of the lecture room
Her move to the redbrick University from a broken home
There cold air lies still across the black space of the open doorway

This brittle heart bears deep pain amongst the bright minds of her class
Under the quiet mask tension rises from her enchained true self
This mask disintegrates to bring the dark flower of depression
Deep inner strength sent self to repair at the mental hospital

In dark days her often reflection on question of who am I
Growing sense in this sparse room as dust mites dance in the Autumn rays
Errors of the past calmly acknowledged in her new inner light
True self emerges in vibrant colours like the Peacock Butterfly

In her smile the vivacious self excited to re-enter the world
With new confidence her social network grows like the rising moon
Golden locks glint under city neon light in the cool clear night
Within her eye the maturity from her trek through depression

Coryli's Journey

Freshly fallen rain forms translucent pearls on rich green willow fronds
Luxuriant field and foliage by the stone path to her house
The plain student furniture in the old open plan timber place
This tranquil environment first nurtured her at her bold return

Walking by she smiles as the Winter rain bejewels her blonde locks
Self newly recovered from the dark crucible of mental crisis
Ready to re-enter our lives as the new bright outgoing self
High expectations after the hard journey from dark depression

Determined to be the warm supporting friend and vivacious host
To understand deep ideas and knowledge at the place of learning
Her growing social net broadly threads between arts and sciences
At the pub English ale and her energetic conversation

With girlfriends home moved to the rambling suburban white stone house
The house-warming party to celebrate her fresh start and new self
Drink and bold music bring alight her web of young and mature friends
At midnight this perfect young woman kissed the imperfect young man

In the high street pub she sits among friends at the mica-top table
Standing close by the shabby drunk spat personal abuse at her
Without emotion her measured words deflate his childish anger
Roughly he lurched into anonymity of the cool twilight

Though her self whole heavy still the challenges of the learning life
Crestfallen in feeling her goals hard to reach with all her talents
Yet honest reflection her essential key to personal growth
In the city gardens new daffodil blooms glow in cool Spring air

I Kept It All In

In Memory of Wayne Jackson (1954-2003), alcoholic
Reference: 'You kept it all in,' song by The Beautiful South, 1989

The black dog of depression presses its paws hard down on my throat
I can hardly breath as its weight crushes the spent air from my lungs
I stop the eighteen-wheeler to leap out amongst the Spinifex
Lights of the nearest town small shimmering stars on the horizon

Desperately I reach for my companion the bottle of beer
Calmed I step up in the cab and drive on in the airy darkness
Almost destroyed the happy gregarious man I had always been
The loving husband and caring father these distant memories

The shadow of my father's death brings the repeated midnight sweats
A grief unexpressed as I hurtle on in frantic activities
I the high achiever yet how empty of meaning these actions
The pain of loss I keep suppressed by alcoholic consumption

In self-consuming acts I am the cruel stranger to wife and child
Christmas 1998 sad self-pity of the drink addict
Lucid moments sharply reveal the hurt I inflict on loved ones
Drink barely buries the memory of the pain in her blue eyes

I cannot halt this terrible spiral down deep to dark destruction
Inner pain accumulated like iron bands across my heart
One more binge renders this body lifeless on the cool kitchen floor
Unheard rain falls gently on the roof as magpies announce the dawn

Kindness for Sale

This cool airy morning late Autumn frost sparkles by World End's Lane
Warm in the maroon Rolls-Royce look-alike with worn fake leather trim
His charming weathered face adorned by the thick wavy golden wig
No job too small though cash-up-front for this well seasoned handyman

Ready service for a deceased kettle or broken cupboard hinge
Even for his elderly clients a charge for chat and a smile
On Saturday night he to play drums in the Grey Bear pub jazz band
A talent in demand as one of the few who could read music

His boastful claim the cards of life had dealt him an old cold hard hand
It is time for life to pay him back in cash for his own pleasure
Glassy surface of the canal reflects rich arboreal splendour
By the towpath a smiling young man admires the fresh buttercups

He the new competition treks away to fix a broken gate
His act of aid elicits warm thanks a little message from the heart
Personal recognition is fulfilment enough this good day
On the towpath he whistles his curly red locks bright in sunlight

The Confession of David Hicks

David Hicks (b 1975), an Australian who attended the Al Farouq training camp para-military training in Afghanistan during 2001, then detained by the United States in Guantanamo Bay detention camp from 2002 until 2007. In April 2007, Hicks was returned to Australia to serve the remaining nine months of a suspended seven-year sentence for providing material support to terrorism.

This stifling cycle of life amongst the manicured city streets
Stealing a car to pay for drugs a hopeless way to gain freedom
A bag on shoulder I depart for clear air of this big country
Work on farms pays my way in footsteps of the self-made travellers

Journey north from splendid flint-dry land to majestic rain forests
A mistake to return home to follow normal suburban dreams
1999 separation from her and our two children
To travel from these sad failures seeded by the restless heart

Will I find myself as the bold warrior a man of pure action?
To the righteous fight with the Kosovo Liberation Army
I travel light with hard black and white ideas of the new recruit
Call me racist but I must believe the cause is rock solid right

Return to Australia cocooned in the hard paradigm of right
Confusion of self buried in the quick conversion to Islam
Thrilling dusty trek to Pakistan to train with terrorist groups
Here is where I feel needed and can earn respect from other men

In Afghanistan surveillance for the extremist Taliban
Captured by militia and sold like a cow to US forces
Attempts to break my mind by brutal physical and mental attack
23 hours each day annexed in solitary confinement

I confess how did the bold adventurer come to this sad state?
Five years away from the sun struck red dust road in this small grey cell
Who is this broken man that huddles on the bleak brink of despair?
I yearn for the smell of horses and dawn dew on the flint-dry land

Ariel

Not her the gentle sylph adorned by the primrose print cotton dress
She's the buxom beauty aboard the silver Balius motorcycle
In Spring sun her journey out of imprisoning expectations
Overhead the agile swift darts about in bold breathless manoeuvres

No longer constrained as the quiet compliant staying home wife
Wreck of the marriage called heavy projected family anger
Yet selflessness to nurture the independence of her true self
Now the open rose of her bright assertive personality

Amongst her inner turmoil still compassion to aid those in need
To each troubled friend her empathic ear and warm consoling word
Meditation brings her tranquil space to grow and discard worry
Under a mackerel sky light rain glints in the bright morning light

The Confirmation

A doctoral candidate attends the first-year assessment

Havana locks and deep glasses of this well worded young scientist
Tense from subtle fear of failure in this serious enterprise
She glad of this early chance to reveal the progress of her work
At twelfth month the road be smooth yet the direction still cloaked in fog

Fine gold locks of this slim family woman the supervisor
Nervously adjusts her hair at the uncertainty loose within
Fear of hidden fault in young motivation or experiment
Warm humanity spills from this dry tradition of assessment

Concrete and Glass

In memory of Campbell Bolton (1988-2005), a young life tragically ended by suicide

First rays of dawn caress the hard concrete and glass of this city
In the hotel carpark Autumn leaves lie by his shattered body
On the neat hotel bed the logical letter his final word
This sadly insular attempt to justify his last action

One year before he a 16 age high flyer with common stress
A gay identity ambivalent to formal coming out
Pressure of an array of heavy questions spiral in his mind
Hot inner confusion calls collapse of his high school performance

Discussing a little with friends but not with his loving parents
Gone the nourishing escapes to the world of imagination
Like a newborn calf the rickety legs of teenage logic
Emotional calculations cast off course by weight of depression

Fear and masculine pride cast addiction to self solutions
To reveal the naked emotional confused truth is impossible
Faulty ideas combined with self destruction the brutal option
The hardy Hakea stands resolute after a Summer bar rain

Reckless

Brian Burke, disgraced Premier of Western Australia 1983-1988

With deep pride he surveys the glittering glass and concrete city
This bell-weather premier fashioned the reckless state in his image
He the strongly built leader with short dark locks and black action suit
Public interest sacrificed for his personal advantage

His father rabid anti-communist of the 1950s
In his bull-destructive political arc lessons for the son
At the death of his father the bell called his explosive career
He to quietly manipulate by one-on-one behind the scenes

A personal political machine to buy your favour or ruin
In production of clay men which is the pot and which the potter?
In clear truth he the hard parent to command their word and action
His hand on each pre-selection, cabinet and committee post

Companies he commanded to donate funds for favoured action
Government he led to blind invest in high-strung business plans
Era of sky-high credit and the '87 stock market crash
His tactic lost the public over 600 million dollars

Now the double-chinned plump oligarch in shades and panama hat
Out of parliament yet still his parental grip on government
White bells of the luxuriant Datura hybrid hang in night air
Thick morbid scent signals poisonous threat of that majestic plant

Present Imperfect

In memory of Sylvia Plath (1932-1963), American poet, novelist, and short-story writer

She the fresh-faced blonde student sits silently on the verdant bank
Across silver water the majestic stone rise of King's College
This gifted young poet of perfect attire yet uncertain of voice
In her eye light of hope for life fulfilled in family and word

Smiling she recalls the explosive passionate embrace with he
Marriage to he the airy poet nurtures their mutual creation
Six years revolved in love until his betrayal broke her bright dreams
She engulfed by incandescent fury at his cruel faithlessness

An energy transduced to poetry of chilling authority
A mind called inward to self-pity and grey depression in grief
Her mind captive to obtuse insularity of the clever
She cast adrift alone on the black treacherous sea of trouble

Mother held distant by letters portraying a perfect daughter
At death of father grief kept shut out in the winter of her youth
This unresolved grief left to fester in the foundation of self
Hidden in her unexpected nervous breakdown 10 years before

Revolving in her mind her attempted suicide back in that dark time
Not amongst her talents the skill to find a non-destructive path
Cycle of her unsteady mind to dark depth on this Winter night
Death the brutal self-act while her children sleep beyond the white door

Through clear sky dawn rays fall gently over the snow-cloaked London street
Bold form of the Mistle Thrush wings silently along the roof line
Under smooth snow Groundsel and Chickweed wait patiently for the thaw
In their room the bright young children stir expecting her ever love

Hubcap

In memory of Sylvia Plath (1932-1963), American poet, novelist, and short-story writer

Fury rides my mind as I skid off the road
I gather ragged thought to swift drive away
Left in the gravel the lone silver hubcap

Take this item as a memento of me
In its sharp curve transformed reflection of truth
Follow the circumference back to our bold start

Its singleness signals my insular reserve
The deep dent marks the dark fault line between us
Detachment from the car calls our last parting

Rhythm of the Heart

*Meg Taylor, Papua New Guinea, from the documentary 'My father, My Country'
(1989). Her father, Jim Taylor, died shortly before this time.*

Forward motion gleams in her dark eyes framed by fine black locks swept back
This youthful high-flyer of the law at work in her young nation
Her finger traces his route through the verdant tropical highland
To re-enact her father's trek by footfall and mind attention

He led the Hagen-Sepik patrol back in 1938
To bring western public government and law to this ancient land
First contact with white-man and his culture to many native groups
His gentle words cast the new future for them to grasp as their own

50 years on still the thick jungle and streams to press through
Challenge of illness and fatigue in the heavy mud climbs skyward
Telefomin the mission town bereft of natural rhythm
Here native culture jettisoned to blankly follow white-man's God

North to Mianmin to see classic wooden pole homes in the making
Sharp arcs of shovels wielded by women road workers in grass skirts
Into the dense forest with unseen tracks to the Sepik River
Success of this journey now perceived in her growing confidence

Turmoil in her mind about the central nature of her father
With her his presence by his work diary and official reports
His identity assessed by elders who had witnessed his trek
Stories of initial conflict later leading to deep respect

Once men were warriors who hurled angry spears and arrows at neighbours
He brought new tools and ways to think to bring schools and the dove of peace
Challenge of this nation to blend best of the new and ancient worlds
Deep strengths from a rich culture that has evolved over millennia

Hidden emotions on camera with her lawyer face in charge
In mind the once young girl in unquestioning love of her father
Reflection by her youthful adult about his deep compassion
To aid her growing recognition of where her life must journey

In her eye the restless push to test her wings in the world beyond
To represent her land in international diplomacy
Heady test of the United Nations amid a sea of talent
In her heart beats the rich complex rhythms of her distant homeland

Bold Heart

Liz O'Shaughnessy (b. 1951), Australian entrepreneur

This bubbly young child glows in her best red dress for the Sunday School
At the main service sound of her mother on organ with the choir
High expectation melded with self belief nurtured by mother
With Aunt Adelaide the joyous love for making glorious food

The black sunless day her mother died when she just newly age 12
Father who saw only his new woman as a vital being
Friction at home due to standing up for her self needs and future
Escape down to the river amid verdant arboreal splendour

Without parental love she desperately unhappy at home
At age 15 leaving home and school to find a city clerk job
In her self belief she evaded harm by drugs and alcohol
At Emerald Hill Market heady aromas amid bright crowds

Among the throng two accepting friendly former alcoholics
She to blossom in confidence under their mature guiding love
Marriage at 21 later cut for her commercial career
This rounded entrepreneur with warm heart and bold theatrical flair

Meticulous Man

In memory of Leon Dousset (1955-2007), veteran linesman for the Australian Telstra company, who tragically committed suicide

Highly meticulous work by this major veteran linesman
Lucid repair of phone faults and maintenance of Melbourne network
A bright mentor to junior staff and respected trouble-shooter
Always a smile and happy word to other staff at the depot

In 2006 rising work load from the aging network
Chained to pressure of fast clear faults but to hard halt standards of work
Then to GPS track of vans yet the heavy mean lack of trust
This quietly proud man was depressed at this dark demeaning changes

Lost on leave without security of familiar job routines
Too much of self silently identified with pride in his job
Despite a loving family his hidden suicide at their home
Beyond the Langwarrin depot his work named around the network

Death of a Salesman

In memory of Sally Sandic (1986-2007) salesman with the Australian Telstra company, who tragically committed suicide

In sunlight her smart stepping with her long blonde locks trail lilting
Happy pleasure as top salesman in the Telstra Como call centre
Her vibrant personality with adorned bright yellow singlet
Fast arc across high sun in broad lead curve of the fork-tailed swift

In 2006 the managers had called white black and black white
Quantum rise in sales targets were set for machines bar our humans
Cold steel monitor of every second in employee days
Manager empathy halted to hatred of subordinators

In giving her best she could not fathom why they asked for the sky
Under cold blast of new supervision her best work seemed wrong
Tears of confusion over failure to reach the new sales targets
Too closely identified with her self as the major salesman

On sick leave lost without the security of working routine
In care of a psychiatrist yet her first suicide attempt
Dull eyes turned nervously down in the cool crucible of depression
Depressed emotion and exhaustion cast her final suicide

Dream Maker

In memory of Belinda Emmett (1974-2006), Australian actress and pop singer

Bright laughter of this young sylph jumps from sands of Umina beach
To put her outer self as singer and television actor
That inner challenge by breast cancer at early maturity
Her dark humour gently brings this tragic predicament to us

Doctor's black diagnosis yet her optimistic prognosis
Deep contemplation of self and her place in the community
Vigorous work on her musical talent and its social role
In this space her balance of self-centred dreams and linking people

Energising flow in sensual connection to he her true love
Pressing on high work despite secondary bone metastasis
Her incandescent joy in marriage to he in 2005
Jolt of heavy hair loss under relentless chemotherapy

Her passionate push back to life in creation of strong vibrant songs
In recorded musical orchids her bright self shines forever
To relax when too tired to resist the final call of death
High in the dusky forest gully bright bell of the Pilotbird

In the Australian Cottage Garden

On lush lawn this seasoned assistant in that caring profession
A fine featured face framed by spiralled locks aglow in Titian red
Perfect through technical knowledge melded with focus on detail
Her lithesome form softly dappled by sun threads slipped through the Hakea

A voice gentle as the susurrus by long back grass in the breeze
Self-effacing lightness amongst patients eases their stress and pain
Lilting motion of Rhodanthe daisies in the wind near her fluid step
Measured strength to extract action from recalcitrant staff

Words of her tragic events fill the shadow of the coral gum
High hope by the Acacia bearing arrays of golden blossom
In her eye sparks the spirit of being as bold as the camellia
Her compassion strong as the arc of the Currawong's flight skyward

The Gift

In honour of Dr Robb De Iongh, medical scientist

Capri blue eyes of his gentle bright smile adorned by short blonde locks
To emerge from the ever dense clutter of academic tasks
Laboratory bound to nurture his bold edge research projects
Astute theoretical knowledge melded with practical hands

Gentle authority rides in his warm organic leadership
Golden empathy in patient guidance of his students and staff
In discovery joy and bright discussion on new directions
His empathic responses glide through experimental failure

His focus on cellular signals that call creation of the lens
To probe the deep mystery of how cells come to divide and change
How the fate of a cell is determined by invisible signals
With high understanding of errors in human development

To future enable the aspirations of stricken families
A young girl to survive the dark weight of congenital error
Priceless gift for a son to heal to marry and be a father
A Red Wattlebird wings across the rising orb of the morning sun

Brief Arc of a Dancer

*In remembrance of Tanja Liedtke (1977-2007), German-born professional
choreographer and dancer*

In emerald eye glows her unique visions of dance in action
As the choreographer to cast complex emotions in dance
On stage the leggy brassy hostess in self-adsorbed beauty
Dance the language of motion to reveal slippery inner truths

Lithesome forms slide adeptly over each other like bright steel cogs
Limbs spin in synchrony with swift bold bounds to claim the open space
Bodies fall about like eucalypt leaves pushed by a highland storm
Wilting forms in slow motion bear the mute sadness of broken love

Late the hour yet her mind restless with future possibilities
To step along the Pacific Highway blind to the starry night
Deaf to the refuse truck slowly clambering at work behind her
Her slim body broken beneath its weight in her premature end

The Lotus Flower

Portrait of a plant biologist

Glittering dark eyes framed by the curved flow of luxuriant black locks
This petite belle smartly adorned by the cream scarf and rich ash coat
The cornflower sky resonates with her faience blue eye shadow
Across the Winter park this bright young scientist glides on two wheels

Past the purple crocuses and yellow daffodils on frosted ground
Nestled in her bicycle basket the small precious orchid samples
She the precocious polymath delving development of plants
To probe the deep symbiotic closeness of fungi and orchids

With a smile her expertise to help build orchid enterprises
Empathy with students to open their young minds to bright futures
Exuberant communicator to bring people together
By still water a Night Heron boldly rises toward the new moon

From her rich garden she gives the beautiful fruits of her labour
Her kitchen brims with the aromas of many foods for your health
Her eye glitters with bold plans for community education
From her heart blooms the lotus flower of empathic compassion

Self-Portrait in Cobalt Blue

She the vibrant buxom belle clothed in the simple Summer print dress
Stellar array of cerise curls fall behind her cheerful fair face
The power of persuasion in her smart open conversation
Her keen skill to help build sponsorship for community events

As the nurse robust words to command the attention of patients
At home the work to let go of strong behaviour to control him
This magnificent struggle to change the self built from her childhood
Upon her wrist the silver bracelet with charms of rain, wind and sun

She labours to assemble the elements to nurture her full self
In yoga to feel each muscle and bone of her physical realm
To begin the journal of self in thoughts of day and dreams of night
Her issues expressed within the self-portrait in cobalt blue

She makes time to peacefully reflect on her inner journey
Each rising thought held to the clear light of the reflective mind
Every embarrassing memory lightly seen as true of self
Empowering self connection under the intense sapphire sky

The Naïve Master

A poem-play in three acts, adapted from Helen Garner's book, 'The First Stone'
(1995, Picador, Sydney).

Actors
* *College Head: The Naïve Master*
* *Student 1: Perdita*
* *Student 2: Erowica*

To begin, set the actors on the reflective stage of your mind

Act 1: At the Party with Perdita

Celebration of his success at Valedictory dinner
This golden year as Master of the old tradition-soaked college
Warmth and vibrant enthusiasm informed his bold new leadership
Fatherly to the students yet loneliness of the outsider

On to the Smoko party of music with dance and alcohol
Her young face framed by the sharp halo of radiant blonde locks
Her vibrant eye adorned by strong eyelash with bold black eyeliner
He and her dance together both unaware of her inner strength

His mind cast with the heady mix of high spirit and alcohol
Released from mind depth the unreformed script of a young man in lust
Entranced by her perfume and sway of earrings over bare shoulders
Allure of her half closed eyes that accentuate the line of strength

Without complaint she removes his heavy hand from her young breast
Yet her swift escape from the room for her anger to his advance
In her head the common feminine script to avoid social angst
She the quiescent victim not to upbraid him from her own power

Act 2: Later in His Office with Erowica

In soft light tanned face and shoulders of this buxom beauty aglow
In the smart black party dress she sat down to discuss her future
He unable to read nuances of her plain words and body language
His lonely thoughts amplified by high elation and alcohol

Of the old school he able only to sense her fine sexuality
In his lair a wish to make this bold young spirit his mistress
Allure of her glowing face framed by sweeping swirled brunette locks
Blind to this feminine strength marked by her bright sensual beauty

This night his gauche grasp of her breast and bleak sexual proposition
Her unspoken repulsion of his unwanted dark attention
Not wishing to upset this man holding power over her fate
His failure to fulfil his duty of care for this young student

Act 3: All to Court

Within his dream at night dark clouds scud swiftly across the old moon
In Black Forrest dark pine pillars stand high over the icy road
By day he cannot forgive the blemish on his moral record
Hollow pride kept him in denial yet the corrosive buried truth

The long Summer of discontent to ferment in the shadows
To protect its reputation the college deaf to their complaints
Sent to court their claim of assault against his of pure innocence
This case unproven yet his reputation crushed by brutal words

Conciliation barred by the steel hard hand of criminal justice
Who paid for a system unable to bring the spirit of the heart?
His wife bright eyes in public yet in private her endless hot tears
The two young women to carry the weight of hard hearted action

At night Perdita dreams of singing to the young college students
They listen smiling to her song about loss of trust with elders
All she wants is to be respected and valued for who she is
Outside a young magpie struts and warbles at the rising sun

Quantum Life

A close friendship of two atomic scientists destroyed by the loyalties and doubts of war in 1941

Bohr

Niels Bohr (1885-1962)

First swallows beat by the bountiful Beech this Copenhagen Spring
I soar about the nucleus like the bold vibrant electron
To jump from one orbital to another ejecting pure light
My suit the rainbow broadcast by a hundred different atoms

Thrill of the myriad airy ideas swirling through this young mind
To a nascent notion mathematics crafts ever precise form
Exposed in blinding glory the inner beauty of the atom
The Copenhagen group I lead with brilliant student Heisenberg

I joust with Einstein by paradoxes in the quantum atom
Yet my deepest puzzle is Heisenberg of 1941
Once great friend how did you appear to me as the cold German brute?
The idea of a German atomic bomb explodes in my mind

Yes I brought my thoughts to advance the first allied nuclear weapon
Yet as you I fought to halt the spectre of nuclear holocaust
Traumas of World War II too dark to bring into fresh light
But to stern heavy cumulus obliterates the horizon

I wrestle 1941 yet dare not tell you my anguish
Tiller to tack recall my first son overboard lost to this world
Complementarity of these old wounds evades this troubled soul
Sound of the first swallow delivers some comfort this my last Spring

Heisenberg

Werner Heisenberg (1901-1976)

On this death bed I do not disquietly request redemption
I the matrix mechanic that sailed secrets of the atom
Add the principle that sets us voyaging in a bright sea of doubt
My guiding beacon I have followed even to treacherous rocks

World War II but all I want to be is the nuclear scientist
This heart hums with hunger to delve deep shadows of the nucleus
You Bohr more German than I in your view of 1941
How could this one meeting destroy friendship deep as the Baltic Sea?

Hazily I query the morality of nuclear weapons
Was it self-doubt that told you I must be a Nazi acolyte?
That incendiary guilt of the atomic bomb is not mine
Yet I am enchained as the amoral pariah of this dark time

How could I claim Unified Field Theory when Einstein not?
This obstreperous ego soars like the moon over savage sea
Yet I push with full success to oppose German nuclear weapons
Now gliding as a twilight neutron through a wistful solar wind

The Crucible of Cancer

Seven poems about the trials and challenges of living with cancer

Crushed

Like past trauma she buried old lovers deep beneath the surface
She as beautiful as Dorian Gray in hapless forward flight
Gilded scaffold of her previous life dim in the twilight now
In her soft centre cancer once more highly like ravenous shark

In her realm compelling grace and compassion for the hurt stranger
Yet civility crushed in the rush to engage a new passion
To be the carer his vibrant eye tells it the essence of love
High on the plum tree two doves circle about in bright Autumn light

Waters of The Heart

Tribute to Dr Ian Gawler, Australian holistic cancer treatment specialist and cancer survivor

In a dark unkempt garden the pool of grief for a lost mother
I the helter-skelter teenage boy riding surf beyond limit
So bright the shimmer on the ocean of my brilliant career
Under the Morning Star walking on water a natural act

Within a heartbeat my star falls lifeless into an arctic sea
This dark shark of cancer crushed mortal bone like tender crab shell
Undertow of grief for loss of the glittering gladiator
Swimming deep water I grasp the challenge to calm the anxious shark

By moonlight this life seems as the endless beat of waves on mute rock
Quietness with Ainslie discards the flotsam of a modern mind
The gentle sea of tranquillity heals my empty spirit
This vision clear as spring water I gift to other lost souls

Searing Spirit

Fine-spun Havana hair forms multifoil blades for swift lift-off
Each night faster than light her calm voyage across the universe
Effortless return by evening ever younger than before
This escape from the comatose capsule of chemotherapy

Cast in black she mourns the helter-skelter of a life no longer
Womanly curves and supple skin mask the deadly campaign within
Patience of the moon her ally against the rushed crush of cancer
Dive deep in bright eyes to touch her searing spirit of survival

Wrestling the Locust

Reference: "Where do you go to my lovely?" Peter Sarstedt, 1966

He my practical friend cannot understand where I must travel
Messages on the answer-tape accumulate like Autumn leaves
I to wrestle the lascivious locust of leukemia
One more bad scan demands this bold trek to inner tranquillity

To dive three thousand fathoms to the grace-state of calm dark depths
Floating in warmth over the junction of massive tectonic plates
Promiscuous pain recedes to flotsam on the distant surface
This broken body tingles with the rise of spiritual strength

Delft Blue

Even the Summer grass whispers my love loves to love another
Unknown neighbours broadcast her rendezvous in the large white building
In her frail physically corrupted form she will leave me
All that remains are the dissonant images of a life shared

The jewel of her smile once obliterated the blackest days
Hot angry tears I cannot express in her gentle presence
Simple pleasure denied of hands entwined on arboreal walks
This sweet space cast by her motion must map to a distant orbit

Her effortless lithesome steps now prisoner of the sterile bed
Voluptuous auburn locks swiftly crumble to barren stubble
My love loves to love leukemia this brutal truth I must own
All that remains is the bold tranquillity in her delft blue eyes

No Complaint

She does not complain of deep lumbar puncture in the bleak hour
Endless wait in grey corridor unseen by the cold eye of death
Doctor's bold orbit curves by each bed as briefly as the comet
Atremble nurse White Rabbit bears no time for tea and sympathy

She does not lament daily destruction of veins by injection
The weight of chemotherapy casts another restless night
Living spirit pushes lethargic body beyond the limit
One more hot flush amidst uncertainty of blood in the basin

She does not grieve the past adorned with high emotional trauma
Eager journalist immersed in frontline conflict across the globe
To follow fresh trail of the dead in East Timor and Beirut
Terror aboard the news helicopter in a fierce fire-storm

She does not cavil at having ever to wear the bright brave heart
No suffering sufficient for her to discard the honest eye
Aloft in majestic gum tree a young magpie sings of bold hope
Stand by the river of her empathy that aids suffering souls

Chemotherapy Blue

In this white room myself held imprisoned as nine fearful hostages
I am the eight guerrillas ready to explode with raw anger
In the grey dawn I see the lifeless body prone on darkened floor
Like Munich ships of scarlet blood drift over the bare grey carpet

After the breathless crisis has passed I slowly resolve myself
Revolving jagged pieces reassemble with less uncertainty
Once more the innocent spirit rises above material woe
In sunlight the wild orchid breathes life into faded memory

The Human Factor in Car Crashes

Thirteen poems to explore the mind sets of people that lead to car crashes, such as by over-speeding, drunkenness, and negligent asleep at the wheel

Silver Star

A rush to death by speeding

Silver star spins fast five kilometres per hour over the limit
Encircled by robust tyre and gleaming body of the new sedan
In the eye of the driver silver star spins dreams of success
Among hard neon the sharp silhouette cruises suburban strip

Too late red light and blood cast violently across the bonnet
Westward lies her broken body anointed by her father's tears
Close by the perfect silver star stands in mute witness to her death
Eastward the morning star slowly draws the cold dawn of the new day

Dead Girl's Curve

Death from drunkenness

This desolate curve raised over the dirty clutter of freight yards
The metal barrier dulled with the exhaust of a thousand trucks
Tarmac and concrete nourishment for small oases of ragged weeds
Mid-curve a grime-encased pole bound in slim wreaths of tattered black tape

Years past the tape held a bright sheaf of twenty one blood red roses
Week on week her bereft parents brought fresh blooms to this acrid site
Here her youthful life crushed by the curse of a drunk freight driver
Ever to pass this slim memorial his eyes hard averted

Road Kill

A mother's grief at the loss of her child

Lilting swing of curved blond locks follows the listless turn of her head
Weary eyes tilt down during dull desiccated conversation
Nervous edge in her voice claims a future of bleak uncertainty
Her baby of sixteen the lifeless blood-soaked body on the kerb

At work rhythm of professional spiel propels her through each day
On the counter her deft fingers show and pack pristine merchandise
Each night on a perfect white sheet the acrid stream of hot tears
Outside measured rise of the new silver moon above her black grief

From ashes of an empty heart her slow rise back into clear air
Now she responds with the almost smile and growing glint in her eye
Return of her assured step floating over the sun-flecked pavement
Close to her heart the locket in memory of her lost loved child

Here Comes My Man

An uncaring helter-skelter life leads to a road death
Reference: "Here comes your man," song title by The Pixies (2004)

Alien to school sent me aimlessly truant to the centre mall
Ever like a circle Sunday drive to the shop strip and return
Smoke bilious from his screaming tyres outside the police station
Dark glasses and cool nonchalance signal the man to rescue I

Only others have glittering partners and majestic careers
I hung in this pitiless existence until glamorous he
His larrikin eye bringer of bold leaving from the stone grey world
Within his space I bash the glass bus shelter into smash palace

Thrill stealing that gleaming sports car to race fast away from town
Laughter as we are airborne over the bridge in fleeting escape
More with as a dull sedan forced off the edge into deep water
I pitiless in prison for death of that loved mother of four

Road Crash Survivor

Guilt of the driver in a high-speed crash

Hung on the grey steel gantry signs name destinations near and far
Below it the chaotic wreckage of two cars and seven lives
Upon the road the jagged body line like terrorists' victims
Behind the wheel blood and my breath ragged as a dying woman

I soaked in guilt as the lone survivor of high-speed disaster
Physiotherapy only bares this disastrous loss of self
Each hot searing ache brands my egocentric humiliation
Too late self-centredness crumples in the face of lethal error

Luxuriant delusions of confidence seem a world distant
Forever this awkward limp not the sensual rhythmic walk
A blooming sense of self-acceptance limits painful memory
Above the steel gantry rises a Sulphur-Crested Cockatoo

Drunk in Charge

Death from drunkenness

Sunday afternoon comfort in the back hotel bar with two friends
Personal demons banished in the languid haze of alcohol
'One for the road' as habitual as the course of the fifteen tram
Yet I in blustery control a world distant from addiction

The car cocoon renders itself on course to take me quickly home
As I speed through the Winter night light pristine snow pressed under tyre
A jolt as the narrow bridge emerges from the cloak of darkness
Screech of metal on stonework before I wrestle the wheel away

Too late three pedestrians crushed brutally against the stone bridge
Sober in dock with empty tears on command of the court sentence
The price for three deaths three years prison at her majesty's pleasure
Not for them I cry but this pitiable self separated from drink

Fading Roses

A novice driver pays the ultimate price

Driving out Saturday night to meet girlfriends at a sassy club
Gleaming at her smart self in the pull-down vanity mirror
Heavy pressure on the accelerator in her bright excitement
Her track the wide dual-lane arterial road with all clear signal

Breast to breast with the black sedan in motion around the smooth curve
Broken down van squats in left lane causing the sedan to veer right
In unknowingness her instant panic jerks the steering wheel right
Rocketing across two lanes heavily into the low brick wall

Scream of crushed metal across tarmac as the small car rebounds back
Heavy rotation rights the car headlights facing into traffic
Rhythm of the engine continues though her neck broken on impact
A grim van speeds past ejects a horn complaint at that obstruction

In dawn rays the bright array of shattered glass by the blood-soaked wreck
For bereaved parents she the amaranthine orchid of their lives
To the police this one more lethal single vehicle accident
By the curve of the road another fading corsage of roses

I Am the Sky

In memory of Lady Diana Spencer (1961-1997) and Emad 'Dodi' Al Fayed (1955-1997), who died together in a high-speed crash

I am the sky she assured I bring rain to nourish the hard ground
The rain drops are your tears he gently replied your heart is broken
He a playboy bachelor ready to become the man in love
Escape to the sun with him yet this unexplained sadness holds her

From the shadows of night pain of a broken marriage emerges
Dawn returns hope and compassion to her energetic spirit
His golden life founded on the love of a resolute father
Day brings fulfilling responsibility to his handsome brow

Luxuriant late dinner at the familiar stylish Ritz Hotel
Quick plan to escape the paparazzi to his private nest
Enveloped in the smooth cocoon of this sleek black Mercedes-Benz
No seat belts for lovers who feel they are beyond mortal stricture

Buzz of paparazzi like bumblebees about the speeding cocoon
Flash of a car close ahead then brake to skid fast out of control
Head on into concrete at one hundred kilometres per hour
Their fragile forms hit the inner skin as two eight tonne behemoths

Pale flowers adorn the rich royal standard across her coffin
Slowly the black gun carriage carries her body past weeping throngs
For he anointed by the tears of his father a private burial
His memorial the bright apartment kept like an Egyptian tomb

Portrait of a Man

*Henri Paul (1956-1997), drunk driver of the car in which Lady Dianna Spencer
and Emad 'Dodi' Al Fayed were killed*

Freedom piloting a light aeroplane over rich hinterland
Each Saturday on the tennis court sparring with a splendid friend
I recall these fingers danced the keyboard as mother sweetly sang
Now they hold a Pastis glass that imbibes I in moderation

Barely I see my form pass in the glass of the revolving door
In secret alcohol buries the pains of a life second best
End of one more brief relationship etches away this manhood
Twelve years past and still only I deputy security head

This sleek powerful Mercedes-Benz rejuvenates I ego
More so these two vivacious lovers that adorn the rear seating
The ivory black car slips through the bright cloak of Saturday night
These paparazzi close behind I will show who is in command

One-four-nought kilometres per hour race to Pont d'Alma tunnel
Brake left to clip the weaving Fiat its drunk driver offends I
Incandescent demons in my hazy head rage for swift revenge
Fast I swing the heavy armoured car right to strongly frighten he

As I jerk back the wheel the cumbrous tail seems too slow to come right
Panic through nought-point-one-seven-four blood-alcohol slams the brakes
Within half a second the vehicle screams straight into hard concrete
Under four hundredths of a second two lovers and I are dead

The driverless wreck spins off the pillar to rest facing eastward
At the famous hospital the beloved princess is pronounced dead
Lone survivor bodyguard only he protection of the seat belt
Now recall I as a man ill met by the cruel winds of fate

Asleep at The Wheel

High pressure lifestyle and lack of sleep lead to death of a couple

Hectic week in work for the pair in love before their planned break
To Colorado for a three-day trip to snow-painted ski slopes
Packing after moonset to rise before the sun this clear Friday
Concentration in traffic when on interstate eighty to Lincoln

Snow cloaked ground by the majestic highway belt across Nebraska
The jet-black Pontiac Grand Am gliding westward fast by the miles
One-two-nought kilometres per hour over the great river Platte
He and she relax on the road in warm comfort with cruise control

After fifteen minutes asleep at the wheel to drift left off road
In left side slide on snow the car veers left onto smooth white median
Jolt awake in fear he jerks the wheel right and stamps the brake hard
Tense panic as the car spins full circle in high-speed skid southward

Tyres soon grip on the eastbound way bearing the vehicle westward
Head on fifteen tonne truck at one-two-nought kilometres per hour
Swiftly the loaded semi-truck crushes the left side of the car
Braking the semi-truck tilts to scream sideways across black tarmac

Within the black Pontiac wreck his dead form slumped over the wheel
She barely a breath blood soaked skin over deep impact injury
Ambulance safely races her to Saint Francis Medical Center
The expert team of hands labours to reform her broken body

On hard white cotton her acrid tears of grief for this shattered life
Reflected in the mirror her broken face and life without him
At the funeral words cast the promise of a life unfulfilled
To her by the desolate highway a cool wind whispers his name

Guilt of the Careless Man

A careless lifestyle and lack of sleep lead to multiple deaths

Perfect Friday afternoon cruising home from distant Warrnambool
The sleek flow of long golden locks across her slender sleeping form
He five hours at the wheel after heavy drinking the night before
Relaxing in warm Spring sun under the endless cobalt blue vault

Drift of the old Holden Calais leftward at the close of his eyes
Awake at the scream of left car panels on steel Armco railing
Too late to see the green Holden Commodore motionless ahead
A twenty tonnes force to crush the soft forms of its two passengers

Rotation of the Commodore to rest with the rear fierce ablaze
Two bodies purified by intense heat of petroleum flame
Inside the Calais dark blood on golden locks and her silent scream
In his broken head cold shock dawns at the obscene ragged carnage

Two forms impelled to the pristine white cocoon of intensive care
Her lithesome motion stilted forever by fractured metal
His damaged face imprisoned by the dark guilt of the careless man
By the desolate freeway roses mark the death of innocence

Shattered Glass

Driving under the influence of acute emotional stress leads to a car crash

White overturned cup rotates loudly on the square golden table
Fawn and raw umber sugar sachets scattered like her fallen dreams
In the empty chair the ghost of her unwanted dark memory
Steps echo hard in the quiet mall as she races from raw guilt

To drive the red nineteen ninety seven Toyota Corolla
Tense heat holds her stomach to accelerate around the blind curve
Light to red as she continues to push the pedal hard floor-ward
Swiftly the high white Mercedes Vito van close across her path

Strong jolt at clipping the van then the high-speed clockwise spin and roll
Her blood spattered on shattered glass amid the smell of burnt rubber
Fear in numbness of her broken body held helpless upside down
Across the intersection the van still after a quarter spin

Unable to run further her tense ragged form laid on pristine white
Beyond window thunder and cold fury of the Winter tempest
Searing tears at the grief driven continual pain of lost self
A different self taps lost inner strength to bring grace to patience

First Daffodil signals self forgiveness of the old brittle she
To accept helter-skelter self no longer need of tight control
In dappled light softly her hand strokes the quiescent feline form
Outside seagulls gently spiral upward on the warm rising air

Side Impact

A young woman driver suffers from a serious crash

In the arc of the 24 hour clock each second to account
Rush in the cocoon of my car without the dusky sun perceived
Press the accelerator to capture time in the outside lane
Impelled too close to the sedan in front when brake lights call danger

Jolting the wheel left the sideways skid at sixty into the tree
Crushing deceleration of my head upon the hard tree trunk
Warm blood drips down my long golden locks as my vision fades to black
White room white sheets cannot assuage racking pain in this broken form

In silver mirror the scarred face framed by long shining golden locks
Yet unfeminine clumsiness of motion and numbness of mind
Dexterity and quickness of thought wrenched forever from my self
Warm tears on the white sheet in grief for loss of the woman I was

With his deep love for me I work to regain part independence
Perseverance with physiotherapy and mental exercise
How he still warmly loves this broken I remains a mystery
Now I see vivid daffodils waving under the dusky sun

The Heart Responds to Terrorism

To honour victims of terrorism and examine the motivation of terrorists in three terrorism events: USA, 11th September 2001; Bali, 12th October 2002; and Jakarta, 5th August 2003

11th September 2001, USA

Four poems in memory of the atrocity 11th September 2001, USA.

Passion

In honour of John O'Neil (1952-2001), former antiterrorist FBI agent and Chief of Security at the World Trade Centre at the time it was destroyed

In fast step this debonair public servant with smart cut suit
His searing blue eyes dance about to gauge all about in the square
This immaculate man on a mission pushes by each obstacle
To some in his path simply the sight of arrogance riding through

On the distant future horizon only he saw Al Qaeda
Relentlessness caught flotsam of slim facts within his steady net
Brashly he assembled fragments of the terrorists' hidden truth
Ever circling the grey short-sighted sharks of petty politics

Key creative tools built to rejuvenate counter-terrorism
Power of the data matrix formed on terrorist explosives
Tirelessly to weave cooperative links with foreign police
His holistic view beams brightly against the darkness of the past

In Yemen the brutal suicide attack on the US Cole
Call in this ruthless man with a bold passion for public service
Barbed Bodine scuttled the bright FBI investigation
As the sun set still his warm compassion for the dead and wounded

To escape the shark pool as World Trade Center security chief
Diligently at work as terrorists' planes broke the two towers
His body buried under concrete and steel as the myriad staff
A Swift spirals upward as the bold bright spirit of this flawed man

Flight 93

*To the memory of passengers and crew of United Airlines Flight 93, who died
September 11th 2001 to prevent terrorists reaching their goal*

Twin engines roar in Boeing 757 lift off after delay
On board from Newark three generations of America's best
Forty six minutes on hijackers swiftly murder both pilots
Their bodies cast on the deck as mere jetsam of the evil task

Hostages sick with fear at murder of their fellow travellers
Twenty four held in first class under the knives of two hollow men
Four smart flight crew herded to the back with nine anxious passengers
That lone bomber their captor in the moments of nascent resolve

Mobile phones bear news of tragic twin towers' aircraft crashes
In the rear gallery the revolt planned softly in guarded moments
Piercing scream at super-heated water cast over the bomber
In his agony stumbles out of the swiftly opened rear door

Silence for the loss of a life even that of the cold killer
Forward the knife men fast retreat in black panic to the cockpit
In boldness the new team presses attack on the barred cockpit door
Panic within the cockpit demands the destructive counter plan

The wheel revolved hard right drives the aircraft to that final dive down
Braced on the bulkhead the magnificent seven recall life lived
Shout as one of when freemen shall stand against war's desolation
The crash driven with the force of a thousand freight locomotives

The incandescent fire purifies the bodies of those free souls
Resolved to ash potent symbol of the few that touched the many
These heroes cast this field by the forest to bar Washington deaths
The rising orb recalls their compassion and bright resolution

Empty Man

Mohammed Atta, 1968-2001, terrorist leader

A childhood in the bleak shadow of daily racial repression
Grey escape to education in the European heartland
To this outsider Muslim injustice seared in high relief
In false logic of the angry man shades of life implode to black

Dulled eyes mark accepting the reality of self-sacrifice
Anger of the like-minded men transformed into terrorist plans
His empty soul empowered by dark dreams of immortality
In this afterlife arrays of virgins sit by your ruby throne

To walk fast by the park blind to call of bird or scent of flower
In his mind vision of materialist paradise beyond life
Days occupied in arranging fellow acolytes for the goal
In Florida to train in aircraft flight with dark deadened heart

Left behind in his bag the long discarded trust and compassion
For the last time the Boeing 767 rose from Logan airport
Flash of knives sacrificed three innocent bodies dead on the deck
Now his mind tranquilly focussed as the cold suicide pilot

The North Tower implodes on impact of the loaded passenger craft
A second crash engenders tragic collapse of the twin tower
After the inferno steel wall columns stand like soft bamboo screens
At the centre of this spiritual place the brass sphere still rises

Lullaby for a Terrorist

A mother foresees the violent life ahead for her child

Sleep now my child for ever restless be the journey of your life
In your sweet trusting eye the violent death of many beloved
Your innocent cry for succour too soon the racist call to arms
Your open spirit to be corralled in the black field of hate

Sleep now my child for ever restless be the journey of your life
Not for your heart compassion to build better lives for the broken
Denied the fulfilment of parenthood a child to bear your spirit
Your short life brief on the world stage fast jettisoned from memory

Sleep now my child for ever restless be the journey of your life
Gentle little fingers will deftly hold cold metal of the gun
Rise and fall of young breast yet to bear the obscene suicide bomb
No grave shall take your body brutally blown piecemeal to the wind

12th October 2002, Bali

Two terrorist bombs ripped through the Kuta area of the Indonesian tourist island of Bali on 12th October 2002, leaving 202 people dead

Three poems in memory of this atrocity

Bali Mon Amour

In honour of the victims of the bombing in Bali, 12th October 2002

Her buxom silky silhouette lilts in the warm morning sun
Translucent halo of short curved locks frame a pensive smile
Fragile inner thoughts brought her to this soft tropical paradise
Now on brown Bali dirt her shrapnel shattered form lies comatose

That gay sultry evening she one victim of the terrorists' bombs
To lie mute amongst hospitalised arrays of battered bodies
Delirious in the noisome airlift to sanctuary Darwin
Under this other tropic sun tears of grief for a broken self

Coalescent resolve to bring battered limbs to the simplest tasks
Hidden scars and creaking pelvis recall a day in paradise
An effervescent life reformed in the crucible of unjust pain
In her clear eye a will to rebuild the community of love

The Racist

A terrorist responsible for the Bali atrocity, 12th October 2002

Incessant gun fire echoes over the dry plains of Dasht-e Khásh
He with Mudjahideen shout hot hate at Taliban enemy
Together in arms he wears the bright coat of God's holy duty
A duty to exterminate the retched Taliban vermin

Fervent ferment against infidels across the wide Pacific
To burn the America flag on betrayal of his Afghan friends
Restless at home in sleepy Tenggulun the East Java haven
Thin mask of religious words barely covers bloated racism

Fall three thousand lives amid twin towers dark cause to celebrate
His obscene plan to murder myriads of dirty foreigners
The old Mitsubishi 300 L heavy with explosive
Innocent milieu of many out that night in Jalan Legian

Casually a finger dials death to trigger that massive bomb
Shards of window glass fall like hard rain on the bleeding burning street
Injured dead and dying bodies lie in ragged blackened arrays
Over desecrated innocence the stand of black smoke rises

The Mask

A terrorist at court, responsible for the Bali atrocity, 12th October 2002

The brimless flat white hat worn in denial of dark forces within
Toward the judges gleams the mask of his innocuous bright smile
In senseless rapid fire loud words hazard a hideous defence
From its dark foundation blood seeps slowly across the wide floor

His arm raised feigns justified support from a higher power
Amidst the public gallery weeps the faces of two hundred dead
Angry tears fall like rain on the sterile barren ground of racism
Out in tropical light a golden plover sings the call of truth

5th August 2003, Jakarta

*On 5th August 2003 a terrorist bomb contained in a station wagon was exploded
outside the JW Marriott hotel in Jakarta, that killed 12 people including the suicide
bomber, and injured 147 people.*

Quiet Comfort

*In honour of the innocent dead and injured in the JW Marriott Hotel bombing,
Jakarta 5th August 2003*

Quiet pride adorns his meticulous professional hard work
He of security guards for the JW Marriott Hotel
This job to aid great care for his beloved wife and son
In his eye the bright hope for a fulfilling family future

She the blind source of tranquillity and peace in their changing lives
Understanding word with strategic advice and perseverance
From her his calm precise motion in the dark crucible of crisis
From his caring warm physical presence she draws quiet comfort

In the dawn she gives him a soft kiss of peace as he leaves for work
Into Jakarta the white Toyota Kijang van races fast
Packed in drums the explosive mute to the violent human end
To drive to destruction another hollow man filled high with hate

Minutes before the lobby abuzz with lively conversation
The adjacent glass-walled restaurant burgeoning with lunchtime trade
By the main glass doors the guards work deftly to screen each visitor
Swiftly the Kijang halts outside to brutally explode in flames

Amidst fire and smoke broken bodies of the six taxi drivers
Four guards dead and he lying amid debris severely injured
Inside shattered glass covers more than one hundred injured bodies
The hollow man blown to dust to swiftly fall forgotten to earth

Supine on the perfect white bed his bloody burnt broken body
Tears fall silently as she listens to his irregular breathe
Forever amid her memory their laughter in the long grass
Beyond glass the pair of golden plovers rise gracefully upward

Corruption of the Spirit by War

Four poems that explore aspects of war

Cold Steel

War in Africa

In the sienna hills young men train not for life but its extinction
Their humanity crushed to create darkly hollow creatures
Cold steel fills the hearts of these bringers of death and dark destruction
In the twilight this Isenguard descends on the quiet village

Cries of the innocent then silence as life-blood pours over dust
Raped and left as dead she crawls raggedly to the quiet river
Escape to South Africa returns tranquillity to her heart
Gentle as air her light voice tells of cruel dark violations

From the act of rape the bright beautiful child at rest on her lap
In her blood course vast arrays of lethal AIDS virus particles
The Prussian blue cloud in her eye marks this sentence to a brief life
In contemplation she steps along sand caressed by sunset rays

Dead Town

A town remains prisoner of its violent past

Dead calm on the main street of this small plain Eastern European town
Fifty years past yet lives still imprisoned as the shadow people
Their shallow forms pressed down by the dark weight of a blood-soaked secret
Through half-drawn curtains eyes stare into distance blind to bright sunlight

Black orchids of avarice bloomed by the fence of the Jewish farm
Whispered tales of the roaming Einzat Gruppen execution squads
Easy slick trick brought this family down to the old outer barn
Through night held in terror by black pistols of the arrogant men

At dawn approaching rumble of the single Shutzstaffel light truck
This warm line of eight innocents raked by the single machine gun
Eight bodies tossed in the unmarked grave behind the blood-spattered barn
Now a verdant field yet that bloated crop of guilt haunts the loveless

Arbeit Macht Frei

In memory of a holocaust victim, only identified as internee 671

Of the death Schutzstaffel I photograph the Jewish internees
This uniform of black splendour demands necessary distance
Only the lens sees their silent terror and sullen submission
In 1944 patriotism stands to feed this dark ego

The plain girl silent before I yet loud warmth of her inner strength
Lithesome promise of bold motherhood palpable yet she just sixteen
The bolt of empathy strikes deep memories of life in sunlight
I can but offer Treblinka with a quick death and nameless grave

In that tumultuous time my personal crisis deepened
Imprisoned in anger by the hard past of those terrible actions
Images of her vital form ever haunt the deep shadows of night
At dawn Skylarks rise high to mock my dark distance from redemption

Abrasive Wind

Training of a Japanese Kamikaze pilot in World War II

Pounding the sienna sand to send the bright red paper kite skyward
As he turns a quick smile and bright laugh toward his loving mother
Step in step they return to the simple low framed Japanese home
Adorned by grey locks of age this is what she hungers to recall

His emotionless eye under the dark Imperial Navy cap
Cast forever in the small black framed photograph close by the stove
The unfulfilled hope that her only son would survive the war
His Sea Captain father lost when his ship sunk in the Sulu Sea

He amongst navel recruits to fight for the divine Emperor
In time out he pounds the wide beach alone to race into grey mist
Mile on empty mile past low wind-swept trees in attempt to escape
Still dark spectre of a distant father so difficult to please

First to push forward at the call for youthful pilot volunteers
Ultimate proof of his worth in this special mission to the sky
Calm eye as his Zero plane aims into the US destroyer
On film the ghost of a dead pilot courted by nine vestal virgins

Braced by the cool abrasive wind she walks the sienna sand alone
Each day at the small shrine she lights incense sticks for her two lost men
From the space of the low framed house her eyes stare at the restless sea
On the hill orphans chatter as she bends paper to make them kites

Murder

To honour victims and explore the mind of the killer, through eight poems.

Cherish the Life

On 28th–29th April 1996 a mass shooting occurred in Port Arthur, Tasmania, in which 35 people were killed and 23 wounded. This poem in memory of the victims

Sunlight barely penetrates the sterile grey depth of each cold day
Memories of my lost only daughter bring hot tears to cold skin
The halo of fine ash-blonde locks to frame her knowing tranquil face
Blind path of a drunken driver closed her nascent life to this brief span

By her grave I scramble to grab meaning of life without her soul
Lost dreams of quiet pride and joy in her bright future fulfilment
Torn away the deep hope of her marriage and offspring of her own
This house ever dark without her gentle compassionate presence

In slow growing acceptance my heart beats once more with emotion
It is I that must carry memory of her brilliant life
Her spirit is with me in the gentle dawn rays of the new day
This gentle breeze carries the floating candle out into the lake

Black Shadow

Dr W.C. Minor, "The Surgeon of Crowthorne", 1834-1920, who murdered George Merrett in 1872

In hidden truth it is I the black shadow betrayer of self
Sleep halts at 2 a.m. by brutal dark internal reflection
Tense wrestled body marks demonic attempts to crucify self
Each night the self tries to kill self in redemption of past error

The killer multiplies in the transferred array of mind demons
Only dawn brings brief relaxed relief before energy of day
Bright sunlight brings this confidence to stay in the civil presents
Stillness to gently paint the restless moors beyond this barred window

I the young surgeon who had been drenched in the hell of civil war
I the murderer of that innocent man projected in demon's garb
Merely redemption by day in the mercy of his young widow
In this release I aid creation of the great dictionary

The history and travel books I read to escape this prison
Calm logic renders unique strategic lists of words in context
To the rational world outside this my timeless contribution
Thunder amidst dark storm clouds low over the moors calms this spirit

Tragedy in the Belanglo State Forest

Between 1989 and 1993 Ivan Milat, Australian serial killer, was responsible for the brutal murders of seven young backpackers in the Belanglo State Forest, southwest of Sydney, Australia

Restless Spirit

In memory of Simone Schmidl (1969-1991), victim of serial killer Ivan Milat

Innocence sparkles in Lupine blue eyes as she laughs with her friend
Glowing smile and conversation mark this beloved bright young spirit
Arm raised and assured shout tell her readiness to leave Regensberg
Excitement to explore Australia with her vibrant backpack

At 8:15 the heat rising on this sultry Summer morning
By railway bus to Casula where she waits at the calm shop strip
Casually he offers her a ride south in his Nissan Patrol
In her German accent the gentle forests of Bavaria

At his direct question blooms the blush on her cheeks to signal trust
Kilometres pass fast by in travel on the wide southern highway
Slow passage through Mittagong then the breathless disconcerting halt
In his steel eye rope and knife to brutally betray her spirit

Deep within the dry sclerophyll forest her body set to dust
By her final resting place the luxuriant Sunshine Wattle blooms
White floral filaments of the majestic Bloodwood gently fall
The susurrant breeze carries recall of her bright restless spirit

Reclaim

*In memory of Joanne Walters (1970-1992) and Caroline Clarke (1970-1992),
victims of serial killer Ivan Milat*

Light mist envelopes the dry sclerophyll Belanglo State Forest
Strong form of the Currawong glides softly through the spare canopy
Lilting voice of the Welsh choir recalls lives from a distant green land
Golden arms of the spring sun reach through grey mist to raise hope anew

The rock that had sheltered Joanne's form adorned by the Welsh dragon
Red array of roses rich in the light of the single candle
Near by the fallen Eucalypt where Caroline's dead form had lain
Dual crosses of the Union Jack nobly mark that fateful site

Amongst the verdant arboreal chaos the priest in pristine white
His strong measured words to reclaim the spirits of the two dead girls
Some comfort to the living marked by the tears of confused grief
Rising skyward the vibrant bright rainbow of Eastern Rosellas

A soft sea mist envelops the old Welsh iron town of Maesteg
The golden trumpets of the Corydalis remember Joanne
In the flight of the Swallow lives her beautiful bold spirit
Here her broken body brought back to rest at peace in rich home ground

On Hindhead height fan of the tall Celtic cross marks God's own country
From here the warm wind takes Caroline's spirit across the green Weald
Below in woodland her bright spirit in song of the Nightingale
Caroline's strong will in the ancient oak of this place of her birth

Milat

Serial killer Ivan Milat (1944 to 2019)

No place to escape in this small house on Junction Road
To face capricious violence of an alcoholic father
A mother's eye held on the continual stream of offspring
Brother rivalry too turns the child in on masculine resource

Softer emotions jettisoned under the constant bombardment
Perfection in his own world creates order within dark chaos
Car and gun ever polished to reflect the searing steel blue eyes
Missing the brakes of humanity in his sociopathic self

A gentle young wife his property to relentlessly control
His red fist to smash the glass table yet black blame to jail her
She set to fail with cloth and brush to maintain a perfect home
Leaves fall to clutter the desolate yard simply to torment her

Few friends allowed to enter this red-brick suburban prison
Bruise-branded body and terrified heart her closest companions
Her desperate escape renders his ego darkly uneasy
Spiritless logic accompanies his black hunt for young victims

Rope, knife and gun laid in place to control the trusting innocent
Hitchhikers bearing backpacks the docile fodder for brutal dreams
Young lifeless forms lie at peace in soft arms of the native forest
Incapable of remorse his coldness captive in the prison cell

Tragedy at Virginia Tech University

On Monday 16th April 2007, a final year student at Virginia Tech University, Seung-Hui Cho, shot dead 32 students and staff, and injured 29 others, before killing himself

Beautiful Balance

In memory of Emily Hilscher (1988-2007), freshman

She a child from the rich gentle cradle of the Blue Ridge Mountains
Her bold warm way to pass through challenging uncertainties of youth
On her new horse taking off at full gallop with bright self belief
Strong empathy for care of animals from the home, farm and wild

Mucking out horse stables with laughter and her heart of happiness
On the leafy forest floor she hears soft steps of foraging deer
She keen on Summer work at the Rose Hill veterinary practice
Growing maturity to care for sick and injured animals

Her passion emerging from the loving haven of family
Winter fun snowboarding with her 'Shredders' friends on smooth white slopes
Jump to the rhythm of her young life in bright vibrant modern dance beats
She master social creator in organising and inclusiveness

First steps on the path to a bright future at university
To study deep science behind animal production and care
In class she the smart creator of social bonds to aid group learning
Among her talents the potential to become a bright leader

This gorgeous young woman with gleaming eye and flowing Vandyke locks
Beautiful balance in talents and passion for the living realm
A compassionate life tragically cut short by that crazed man
Her still body gently comes home as mountain blue birds sing her name

Engineer of Love

In memory of Kevin Granata (1961-2007), faculty member

A child of Toledo the glass city with his loving parents
At school emerged his gifts of the mind welded to sport and humour
Physical and electrical engineering his higher learning
Nascent thoughts of how to engineer aid to ones in deeper need

His move to Virginia Tech to support his high research vision
Now to understand the dynamic rein for reflex of muscles
Rising star in applying this to motion in cerebral palsy
To encourage cooperation among different research experts

To students his office often open for deep lucid advice
Empathy and patient care of students in their learning journey
Guiding research students to grapple the big questions of science
In his bright eye the engineers' verve to seek total solutions

In his words for his family the orchid of devoted love
Father and friend to his children to promote their personal growth
His depth of knowledge balanced with a warm creative vision of life
Complex ideas translated to bright vibrant words as clear as glass

This handsome man with neat ginger moustache and blue eyes aglow
Gentle push of his positive life cut short by the crazed gunman
Strong Spring hues reflect in the high glass arc of the main library
By silver water Green-tailed Towhees call among arboreal arms

Desperate Believer

Seung-Hui Cho (1984-2007), who murdered 32 people at Virginia Tech, 16 April 2007. Title taken from the song 'Straight Lines', by Silverchair, 2007

In this immigrant family I the boy of bright male born dreams
Yet secretly abused by an adult of ever smiling trust
I reinvent as the hard boy who will never trust another
Emotions are for others as I hide in my new hardened shell

Complete with poor self-assurance I avoid deep social contact
Comfort of this shell through the trials from child to adolescent
Tension to abortively try to communicate self with girls
Even to this self I cannot express my true inner feelings

I am the desperate believer in the fulfilment of self
With hidden high stress I walk the straight line of my insular life
I feel it cracking like thin Blacksburg pond ice in the new Spring thaw
Too self-centred to believe sharing thought with another can help

Cracks grow in the shell as I fail to reach my prized goals in this life
I am jealous at the gentle successes of other students
I hate their blossoming careers and partnerships of the bright heart
Lack of social skills pushes me back to the prison of my shell

To seek solution in the dark distorted mirror of my mind
Heat spirals inward as the ragged fault line in thought arises
In creative writing I project red raw self hate on nameless peers
Counselling is futile as I deny all failures of the self

Yet the pain of failure invades my core like a strong black cancer
In the darkness finally a foolproof brutal plan of action
To resurrect my image as a real man through self destruction
My deluded ego demands the brutal deaths of thirty-two

With two semi-automatic pistols I now feel a real man
With all emotions shut down it is time to make my brutal mark
Victims fall at my selfish will before the last shot kills this I
Outside empty arboreal curves yet to bear the life of Spring

Appendix

Mental health helplines

If any of these poems bring up related difficulties for you, please consider calling your relevant local mental health helpline. Listed below are selected helpline numbers for Australia, New Zealand, United Kingdom, and the USA.

Australia

Name of service	Purpose	Phone number (availability)
1800RESPECT	National sexual assault, domestic family violence counselling services	**1800 737 732 (24/7)**
Lifeline	Crisis counselling, support groups and suicide prevention services	13 11 14 (24/7)
Blue Knot Foundation Helpline	For adult survivors of childhood trauma	1300 657 380 (9am-5pm AEST/ 7 days a week)
Beyondblue	Information and referral to relevant services for depression and anxiety related matters	1300 22 4636 (24/7)
The MindSpot Clinic	For people with stress, worry, anxiety, low mood or depression	1800 61 44 34, AEST, 8am-8pm (Mon-Fri), 8am-6pm (Sat)

New Zealand

Name of service	Purpose	Phone number
Are You OK	family violence helpline	0800 456 450
Shine	confidential domestic abuse helpline	0508 744 633
Depression Helpline	to talk to a trained counsellor about how you are feeling or to ask any questions	0800 111 757
Lifeline		0800 543 354

Samaritans	0800 726 666

United Kingdom

Name of service, purpose	Phone number
Sexual Abuse Centre	0117 935 1707
Women's Aid National Domestic Violence Helpline	0345 023 468
Samaritans: Confidential support for people experiencing feelings of distress or despair	116 123 (24/7)

USA

Name of service	Phone number
National Domestic Violence Hotline	1-800-799-SAFE (7233)
National Sexual Assault Hotline	1-800-656-HOPE (4673)
National Suicide Prevention Lifeline	1-800-273-TALK (8255)
NDMDA Depression Hotline – Support Group	1-800-826-3632